Instagram Marketing

How to use Instagram to generate leads and sell products and services.

Intro

Instagram is the fastest growing social network.
Over 800 million people use Instagram every month.

This is a huge opportunity: in fact, according to Statista, in 2018, products were sold for over 6 billion dollars on Instagram against less than two billion dollars in 2016.

This is an incredible growth that shows no sign of stopping: brands receive much more activity on their Instagram channel - on average 4 times more, and 14% of users are interested in buying a product directly from the app.

Whether you want to sell a product or a service, or just improve the visibility of your brand, Instagram is the platform for you.

In this book we will explore the methods and strategies for marketing on Instagram and seeing results, without wasting time and money on tests and bankruptcy strategies.

The focus of this book is not on vanity metrics: the goal of marketing on Instagram is to sell.
Accumulating useless followers, random likes and automatic comments doesn't bring money. Let's leave it to others.

Contents

Intro 2

Contents 4

Step 0: What do you really want? 6
   Don't underestimate the little ones 29

Instagram Ads 34
   Lead Generation 36
   Better than Google? 38

Instagram Stories 39
   Link in Stories? 41

Growth Hack: Reach new followers for free 42
   Regram! 47

And from online too! 52

Instagram Analytics 57

Instagram and Shopify 59

Automate Instagram 60

   How does it work? 61
   Configure your target 63
   Configure actions 65

Case Study: Mercedes GLA 68

Case Study: AirBNB 69

Disclaimer 71

Step 0: What do you really want?

Instagram is therefore the fashion of the moment. This is an incredible opportunity, but it is necessary to have clear ideas before launching.
Signing up for Instagram and starting posting without a goal won't get you anywhere - unless your goal is not to have a profile with so many posts!

It is therefore necessary to understand, from the beginning, where you want to go with your Instagram profile: how many sales you want to generate, how long you want to get there, what kind of commitment you expect to face.

Define these goals immediately.
They must be measurable goals, of which you can have a clear and objective vision. And they must be specific.

The definition of a clear and precise objective is fundamental for two reasons:
- Responsibility. You will be responsible for achieving - or not - your goals.
If you don't give yourself a goal, you don't risk failing. And if you don't risk failing, you will never be encouraged to do better.
- Effectiveness. Through a series of optimization strategies we will be able to increase the effectiveness of every element that comes into play in sales on Instagram. We can increase this effectiveness, but only if we have a goal: otherwise we work blindly.

Our goal can be monetary (for example, generate 10 sales per day via Instagram), but not necessarily.
We can also give us a different goal, for example to reach a certain number of people at each post, or get subscriptions to our mailing list, or even get some B2B contacts for a telephone follow-up. We can

also be creative and use Instagram to reach newspapers, or even as a channel to put our product in the hands of thousands of influencers.

In short, the goal depends on us, but we must have one and work in the direction necessary to achieve it.

The Instagram profile

Profile care is essential.
Instagram is a social network based mainly on photos. The spaces to place text are limited, and the attention that these texts receive is even more limited.

So it is essential to make the most of them.

The most important section is certainly that of the personal profile: here we have a bit of space that we can use to talk about ourselves or our company.

It is important to be brief and concise. Emoji or hashtag is often used to make the profile more emotional and empathetic without getting lost in long texts that few people will end up reading.

The link to our site is fundamental, which we can set in the URL section.

If we have an ecommerce, this will also be our call to action. It is, in fact, the only external link that we can set on the Instagram profile, which otherwise does not allow links either on the photos or on the personal profile.

We can also use a service like LinkInProfile.com to create a page that can send the visitor back to multiple links.

As for the content of our profile, it is good to use a profile photo that represents us: companies tend to use their logo, while people or personal brands take a picture.
The photos to be shared are essential to entertain visitors and, above all, to reach them during their normal navigation.

Let us therefore commit ourselves daily to the creation of effect photos or videos, capable of arousing emotions and feelings in those who look at them.

Content and context

Content is the key to a project's success on Instagram.
It may seem trivial and obvious, but let's not forget it. Even once you reach 1,000, 10,000 or even a million followers, the content will remain all we have to communicate.

If you create random content, you will attract casual people, passengers. This is not what a company needs, which must, sooner or later, convert these people into customers.

It is therefore necessary to create a strategy of contents that can lead us to the achievement of the objective we have defined. To do this, we need to consider another variable: the context. That is, every single content, every photo we publish, every word in our biography, plays in a team with all the other contents.

The context creates a meaning in what we are doing, bringing the customer, even indirectly, to action.
The context is what allows us to bring our content to the attention of the right person, at the right time. Because this person will be attracted by the context, not by the single content.

To create context on your Instagram profile, you must answer the questions:

- Who
- Thing
- Where is it
- When
- Why

Strange is it?
Let's see what it means right away.

Each content must have the viewer well defined, ie who will see or use the content itself; the meaning of the content itself: what do we want to communicate?
We then define where and when we want to reach this person.

Last, but most important, is why. So, how this content plays within the context we want to create.

I want more engagement

Engagement will not bring profits directly, but it is still very important to keep our customers, or potential customers, close to us.
They always have to know who we are, what we do and why. What better way than making them participate in our campaign on Instagram?
In this way they will also contribute to building our visibility, combining business with pleasure.

Use original photos
Those who spend a lot of time on Instagram see thousands of photos every day. It is therefore essential to publish something new, original and that does not seem recycled.
The stock photos are therefore to be banned, even those provided by premium services.

Publish relevant photos
Whenever you post a photo, you need to be clear about who you want to attract. Who are the people who will see it? How can you capture their attention with an image?

Ask users to participate
We have seen, therefore, that it is important to make the users of our initiatives participate. The easiest way to do it? Ask!
The thing that most increases user engagement is to ask for it explicitly. Let's comment or ask to Like the photo! The results will come soon.

Use geotagging
When you post a photo on Instagram, you have the option to add a geographical location to the photo. A sort of hashtag that is mapped onto a map.

Did you know that photos that include a geographical location receive 79% more engagement on average than those who do not?

This is possible because the photo will be visible not only to those who follow you, but also to all the people who search according to your area of reference. This technique is essential especially if we are organizing an event!

How to do it? It's very simple: when you're about to post a photo, click on "Add Location," right after the button that lets you tag people.

At this point you will have the possibility to select a geographical position that you want to link to the photo. Note: it doesn't necessarily have to be your real position! Use your imagination!

Add a description to the post
Often this technique is underestimated. The description of the photos is, in many situations, considered superfluous or useless, and most of the pages write the bare minimum and then insert the hashtags directly.

Nothing could be more wrong. Instagram gives us up to 2200 characters to be included in the description. And we have to use them all, in the right way.

By default, the user will only see the first three lines: we use our copywriting technique to immediately capture attention. In the following lines, instead, we can go into a very complete description of what we want to convey.
Let us remember to use this space to include, once again, a call to action and then ask the user to perform an action.
Put the hashtags in the comments

Exact. You have 2200 characters for the text of the photo. Use them for this.

Nobody cares what hashtags you used: these are used to make you find, not to communicate. Enter the hashtags in the comments, instead of in the description, to have a cleaner post.

Moreover, you will have the possibility to insert more hashtag: Instagram, in fact, limits to 30 only those inserted directly inside the post.

Also, remember to use specific hashtags - #instagood is very popular, but it has no real meaning: the engagement brought by #instagood visitors will be minimal.

Plan your posts

I am not referring to an automatic system for planning the publication - which we will discuss later.
Simply, you need to publish constantly and continuously to maintain the engagement of those who follow you.

People or companies with more followers tend to post a lot. It's not casuality.

A good average, sustainable but not too heavy, is to publish one or two photos a day. We will see, in fact, that each photo remains visible only for a limited period of time - of course, it will be published forever, but few people will scroll their bulletin board enough to see it.

Create at least 5 stories a day
Really? So many?
Yes, but it's not that difficult. You can take photos, videos, or both. And, even if they have to be quality, you don't have to worry

about it too much: even life scenes or daily work will work.

Create one live per day
This technique is also particularly effective.
Live on Instagram is still little used, so transmitting live now can give you a real boost.

In fact, while you're live, your account will be visible to all your followers in the story panel! This will give you a lot of visibility and will not fail to remember you.

Put your face on it

Instagram is a very visual social network, and leverages a lot of emotions. Don't hide yours.

On average, the photos that represent people receive 38% more likes.
If you are a company, it can be a bit more complicated than expected, but don't miss the chance to let your staff know about customers: very often dealing with people of flesh and blood is reassuring and creates a closer link with your products.

Here are some ideas:
- A simple photo of the staff at work
- Photos of employees outside working hours, perhaps at a company party or some special event
- Photos behind the scenes, to show customers how a product is made. Very effective especially for handmade or high-

tech products, where there is a strong curiosity.
- Photos of animals at work! Your employees' puppies will be happy to help you.

Work with influencers

The influencer-marketing industry on Instagram is worth over a billion dollars.

There are influencers able to earn over half a million dollars per post, and the average value of a post is $ 500.

But who are the influencers?
These are people who can spread our message and, literally, influence a certain amount of people in choosing a specific product. An influencer can deal with fashion, like another car or electronics.

This is possible thanks to the relationship that the influencer has created with his fans: sharing interesting and emotional content, the followers see the promotions as personal advice and not as advertising. It is however important to choose an influencer with a target audience, going to study the past collaborations that a particular influencer has had, and the results they have brought, at least in terms of engagement.

Our brand can greatly benefit from collaboration with these people: let's contact them directly on Instagram. The most famous work with communication agencies, which we should contact to obtain our publication.

How to choose an influencer right?
Let's get into the technician now.
Let's go to BuzzSumo.com, click on the "Influencers" tab and enter the keywords that interest us.
BuzzSumo will look for us a list of influential people in that sector, with lots of followers and engagement counting.
After finding an influencer with many followers, we need to verify that these are real.

We log in to SocialBlade.com to do this verification: we insert the name of our influencer and SocialBlade will show us the relative statistics.

So let's see the engagement rate, or how much our influencer is able to get hold of his followers. This value is very important because a very low number indicates in all probability that our influencer has bought the followers.

An engament of around 5% is sufficient: it is practically impossible to reach figures over 10%.

We can also see the growth statistics of our influencer: slow and steady growth is a good clue, while on the other hand fast growth, perhaps followed by a slight loss of followers, often suggests that these have been purchased and therefore have no value.

To have a ready-made service instead, we can use Shoutcart.com. Shoutcart is a very original idea: it is a real marketplace for gaining visibility through influencers.

After registration, in fact, we can directly insert some keywords for which we are interested in promoting, and Shoutcart will direct us to the best influencers in that niche.
We can then proceed with the order of the shoutout, or the sharing of one of our promotions, through the website by paying directly with PayPal.

Furthermore, Shoutcart allows us to have all the influencer parameters available in one place, allowing us to save time by performing our due diligence in a single portal.

A quick tip: ShoutCart will also allow us to buy timed posts, for which our influencer will work only for one or two hours.

This may seem to be a particularly disadvantageous condition, but it is not. In fact, about 50% of the interactions in a post take place in the first hour, to reach 60 in the second and only 80% in the remaining 23 hours of the day.

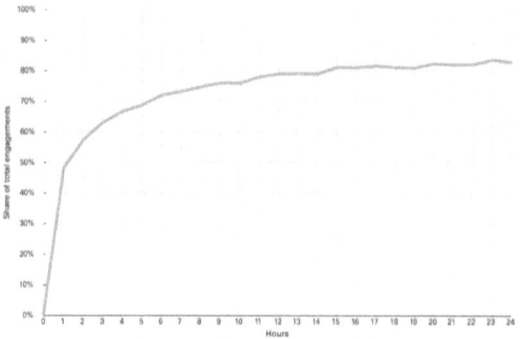

So, we are able to buy at a fraction of the price, a good share of the effectiveness of the post.

So it's better to publish two or three posts from an hour rather than one that lasts over time!

Don't underestimate the little ones

When we talk about influencers, people with millions of followers come to mind, able to reach practically an entire nation with a single post.

However, as you saw on Shoutcart, there are thousands of micro-influencers, able to reach a few thousand people anyway. These influencers have, on average, a better engagement rate, as you can see from these Markerly charts.

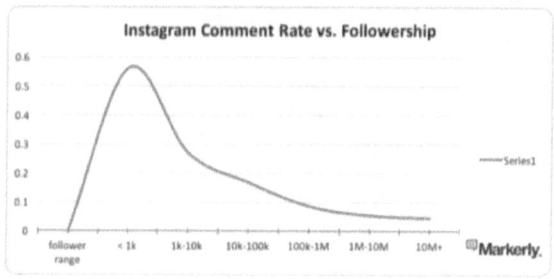

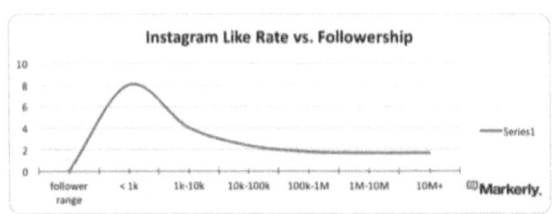

It turns out, therefore, that the more the followers increase, the slower the engagement rate. But the price increases!

Of course, a 2% engagement on 10 million followers is still a huge number, but with the same budget we can collaborate with 1000 10k follower influencers and get much better results - even 100%!
How is it possible?
Micro-influencers have a great influence on their followers.
Just think of the biggest influencers in Italy and in the world. It's basically about celebrities, public personalities who are famous regardless of their activity on Instagram. Thus, an important part of their

followers is not really interested in their content, but follows them because it has known them elsewhere.

This does not happen with micro-influencers: as we have seen, as well as our goal is to attract target customers, few but good, the same is for them. The engagement rate is therefore much higher and often these people are points of reference, perhaps local or in a small but very specific niche.

Customers at work

Generating content daily can be very expensive. It is not easy, in fact, to take photos and shoot videos that are always different, with different products in new environments.
The solution is very simple: let's make our customers work!

We can hold contests in which we ask our followers to take pictures in which they use our product or show some features.

We are giving away one of our products or simply the possibility of being chosen for a re-sharing: Our users will appreciate the additional visibility, and this will allow us to always have new contents to share on our page at no cost - or almost.

How to do this?

It's very simple: it is often enough to define a hashtag to identify the photos generated by the customers who use our product, for example #myexamplewatch can identify photos of an "Example" brand of watches.

It is important that this hashtag is truly unique and identifying: if we choose commonly used words, we lose the ability to create brand awareness and visibility through customer posts; furthermore, we complicate our lives when we have to go and look for photos to share.

Instagram Ads

Advertising is obviously the standard method for growth on Instagram. As well as on Facebook, even on Instagram we have the opportunity to sponsor our posts to reach people who still don't follow us.
We are able to select our target with extreme precision by using the same Facebook control panel, Facebook Ads Manager.

In fact, during the writing of the announcement, Facebook will ask us to link our Instagram account

A very interesting possibility is the advertising in Instagram Stories: it is in fact possible to publish our stories also as promotional messages, allowing us to reach target people directly while they are watching the stories. In fact, our history will appear among those that the person is looking at, and it is a very direct method to catapult the potential client directly into our world.

Lead Generation

One of the new features of Facebook Ads is that of lead generation.
In fact, Facebook already knows the user's email address, and is therefore able to provide it without the need for him to enter it manually.
This lead generation technique is extremely effective and easily converts, because it lowers the user resistance barrier: now it just needs to click a button, and we will automatically receive the email contact.

The user does not leave Instagram and lives an experience that is completely simple and integrated with navigation.
How can we use this new promotion opportunity?

When we create a campaign on Facebook, we can now choose "Lead Generation" as a goal for the campaign.

We just need to create the email and thank you request screen in order to receive this information with a single click of the user!

At the end of the campaign, we export this data to a CSV file that we can later import into our autoresponder.
We can also automate this process if we use one of the supported services, such as MailChimp or SalesForce.

Better than Google?

Instagram Ads and Google Adwords are undoubtedly the absolute leading online advertising platforms. The choice of the first or the second is strictly connected to the real goals you really want to complete.
Of course, one does not exclude the other, given that many companies use Google Adwords to intercept the needs of informed consumers and Instagram Ads to increase brand awareness.

In this case, there are many companies that implement an integrated strategy in relation to customers interested in buying, customers unaware of products ready to be launched on the market and new customers to be captured. Instagram Ads, however, in terms of cost per click, has lower costs than Google Adwords, where the role of keywords ultimately presents the account.

Instagram Stories

Instagram stories are, in any case, very important to involve our followers.
The fashion of the stories has now exploded and a large part of the users of Instagram looks at them very willingly, overcoming in some cases the normal posts.

Furthermore, the very functioning of the stories, allows us to push users to take advantage of our content more often: while the posts are there, and they will remain there forever, the stories disappear after 24 hours and it is therefore our followers' task to follow us constantly and interested so as not to miss any updates.

However, we take into account this deadline, which can also represent a limit. Stories are often used by public figures for brief and informal communications.

Finally, let's not forget the possibility of using hashtags even in stories: the same rules that we used for posts are valid!

Link in Stories?

Who uses Instagram will surely notice that some accounts have the possibility to add a link, a real web link to their stories.
This method is extremely effective, but it is not clear who can use it and who cannot.

We see it immediately: in fact, it is enough to have over 10 thousand followers to have the possibility of adding a call to action to our stories on Instagram.

Growth Hack: Reach new followers for free

It is not necessary to invest huge capital when we want to grow on Instagram.
In reality, there is a method to reach our customers at no cost.

Following this method, you will be able to get 50+ followers a day (and probably even more) without spending a euro. And the speed of this system increases as your follower's increase, so don't give up right away!

First of all, you need to find your competitors who are already on Instagram.
Who are the important people or companies in your sector that your potential customers already know and are following?

It is very simple: access Instagram, then search for a relevant hashtag in your market.

Then open one of the photos in the "TOP POST" category. These are images shared by people with a high following, or who have had high engagement.

We also want to replicate this result: why not reach the same people?

Try to think about it: these are people definitely on target, because they are already interested in the product of our competitor, and they are active users on Instagram, who besides being able to become customers will also help us gain visibility with new people.

So, let's open one of these photos with high engagement, and let's look at who shared it: in all probability, it will be a profile that works in our market, with a following of followers that is very important and interesting for our purposes.

We then click on the number of followers of this profile: here we will be able to access the list of people who follow the profile.

If they follow the profile of one of our competitors, who offer a product or service very similar to ours, they may decide to follow us too.
So let's see: let's start following these people!

It's so simple, but it works.

You can do the same thing even with influencers who already know how to have a good correlation with your market!

How many users can you follow with this method? Don't worry, over 50 every hour.

Instagram does not want a single profile to "bother" a large number of users. However, this number, although not officially declared, appears to be of 7500 people.

"7500 people" is a large number, and you will hardly reach it by mistake. But even if you have to do it, don't worry: stop following some people and resume the procedure.

If you start following too many people, too quickly, Instagram could also block the use of the "Follow" button.
You don't even have to worry about this: it's not permanent damage and your account is safe. After a few hours, this feature will be unlocked again and everything will return to normal.

When you start following these people, many of them will decide to start following you. So remember to post interesting content, otherwise, you may have a large following, but unused!

Regram!

If you are already active you surely know what is meant by Regram: it is the equivalent of sharing a link on Facebook.
Instagram, however, does not provide this possibility natively. For this reason, what is often done is simply re-sharing the same photo by tagging the profile that initially shared it.

This practice, often not appreciated by some companies, is very useful and plays in your favor if the content is created correctly.

What is the growth hack that affects the regram? Simple: when your photo is published by another user, simply go and see who has interacted or commented on the photo, and starts following these users. I'm interested in your content - they just don't know it yet!

TIP: you can use a watermark in your photos. In this way, those who make a regram without tagging themselves will still contribute to spreading your brand. Remember, however, that it should not be invasive graphics and should not clash with the photo!
You can also use online services like Watermark.ws to add text or a logo to your content, whether it's photos or videos.

Make group

On Instagram, something very special can happen: you can collaborate with your competitors to reach both customers.
Such as?
It's very simple: you will each be an influencer for the other.

You can then register your competitor's posts, asking him to do the same. Or you can even share a photo of your product, or use its hashtags. Obviously, this must be reciprocated!

It could also be a good idea to organize a joint venture contest, to offer customers even two products of their interest.
In this way, you will have both the chance to grow on Instagram, to the benefit of all.
Then it's up to you to convert faster than the competitor!

From offline to Instagram

Have you ever thought about how you can turn your users' offline into interactions on Instagram?
This is a technique that is too often underestimated, but which allows it to grow rapidly on Instagram by leveraging an already established offline customer base.

Here are some ideas for bringing your customers to Instagram through an offline medium:

- The base: the Instagram logo with your contact is a relatively widespread, but still functional, system for bringing people from offline to Instagram.

You can let your customers know you're on Instagram with flyers, billboards, business cards if you work in a local context. Otherwise, if you work with customers remotely, you might consider buying a stock of personalized envelopes with your own graphics that, among other things, indicate a reference to your Instagram profile.

- Product hashtag: it is certainly a more aggressive technique, but one that lasts and brings results over time.

Internationally renowned companies such as Olympics, Adidas, and Nike have used this technique to grow on Instagram using their - huge - offline fan base.

- Encourage customers to follow you. Tell them about the possibility of winning a prize every month with the contests you organize, or the possibility of being shared on your page. If people start following you, return the favor with something they care about!

And from online too!

It may seem trivial, but a large number of companies do not adequately communicate their presence on Instagram.

Remember, therefore, to let all your users know that you are also present on Instagram.

Enter your Instagram profile on Facebook, on your website, in the signing of your emails and in general wherever you can: people will not go looking for it spontaneously, it is you who must reach them and let them know that you are there.

On the website, you can even create a gallery directly from your Instagram profile.
Shopify, for example, provides a content block that can do it completely automatically!

This is a very interesting technique to have content always new and updated on the website, without having to do it manually.
Moreover, those who click on one of the photos will be redirected to your Instagram profile and will have the opportunity to start following you there too.

Integrate Instagram into your products

This is a technique that not all companies can use, but which is extremely powerful in cases where there is a way to apply it.

Have you ever played a game on the phone that works with a credit system, like coins to spend on some objects that help us progress through the plot?

Apps4Life has devised a simple but extremely effective system for converting users of their games into followers, to whom they can later learn about new releases.

The system is very simple: reward users with (virtual) coins, if they follow the Instagram page. Thus, these players will be

encouraged to follow the page in exchange for an advantage within the game.
But if they have downloaded the game, it is clear that they are target people: it is therefore not a tactic to force the growth of the page, and even if we use virtual coins as a bargaining chip, it is still a method of growth perfectly organic and in-target.

We find a way to integrate this type of promotion into our business: for example, if we are a restaurant or a local store we can let those who follow us receive a discount code via Direct Message that will entitle them to free coffee or any kind of gift we can offer.

We can then automate these Direct Messages via Stim Social, as we will see later in this book.

Finally, if we manage an eCommerce, we can use the same technique as the discount code, but not only!

We can, therefore, integrate Instagram into our sales channel, also sending promotions over time via DM.

This turns our follower's Direct Message box into a sort of email box to receive newsletters. But much more direct!

Instagram Analytics

There are several tools to analyze the performance of our posts on Instagram. Among these, the most famous is certainly Sprout Social.

Sprout Social is a very interesting tool, which we can use to automate the publication of content over time - not just on Instagram.
But the most interesting feature of Sprout Social is not this: it is the possibility to see the performance of our posts, even those not planned, to optimize our behavior.

Among other things, we can assess the effectiveness of every hashtag we use or of any geographical location if we are working in a local company.

This feature is very interesting because we can bring a large number of improvements to our posts which, added together, will manage to create a sensible improvement to our performance.

Instagram and Shopify

If you work on an eCommerce and want to promote products on Instagram, you might consider using Shopify as a platform.
Shopify and Instagram have a unique functionality: the "shoppable" posts, or the possibility of buying a product on Shopify, directly from a post on Instagram.

If instead, you want to integrate a direct purchase feature, without using this integration - which is still in beta testing and not available to everyone, you can evaluate LikeToKnow.it; a service that can link a photo to a product on any eCommerce.

Automate Instagram

Stim Social is a very special service: it allows you to automate the activities of our profile on Instagram to make it grow without our intervention.

Instagram is becoming more and more important and organic growth of your profile is very demanding. There is the option to buy followers at very low prices, but this has no value other than the aesthetic one.

Stim Social, instead, allows us to get on Instagram contacts of people interested in our product or service, and to reach them in a completely automatic way.

How does it work?

Stim Social is able to automate our activity on Instagram in these three ways:
• Put Like to the photos of the people on target
• Start following the people on target
• Write a message to new followers

As we see, the key to everything is to deal with people potentially interested in our sector.

How can we do it?

Stim Social allows us to select our audience based on some parameters.
• Accounts followed
• Hashtags used
• Geographic location

So, to sum up, Stim Social will create our target based on the people who follow particular accounts, use hashtags defined by us and live in a certain place, and on these accounts can perform actions to follow them, comment on their posts and add a Like.

Configure your target

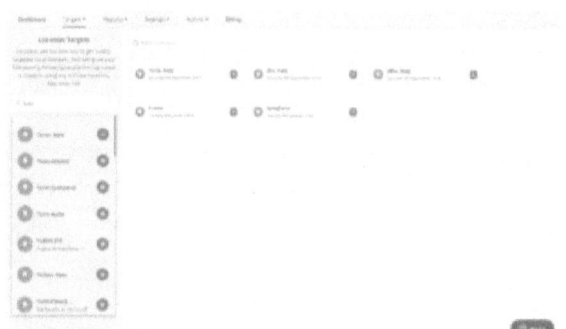

The screens to configure the target are extremely simple.

• Targets> Accounts allows you to add a list of accounts followed by people who can be on target. So let's not add the target people to the target, but the accounts that can be followed by the target people!

• Targets> Hashtags allows you to select which hashtags the people who are interested in our service use. Stim Social will interact with these people.

• Targets> Locations allows us to establish a geographical location for the people on target. Very useful for local marketing of commercial activities.

Configure actions

We are almost there!
We must now configure the actions we need to take on the target audience.

Let's go to Settings> General to configure the speed with which these actions are performed and the limits.

In particular, the particularly important limit is the one defined as Follow Limit and the corresponding Limit in the Unfollow section.

Since Stim Social will start following people on Instagram hoping for follow back, the process is as follows:
1. Stim Social follows these people until the Follow Limit is reached
2. Stim Social will start to stop following these people until they reach Unfollow Limit
Therefore a spread that is not too high between Follow and Unfollow Limit guarantees us a more constant following counter and helps us to have fairly constant growth.

Finally, from the Stim Social Dashboard, we can enable and disable the actions to be performed: we can, in fact, deactivate the Follow or Like function based on our preferences.

Write an automatic message to new followers

The last topic, very important if we use Instagram to find customers, is the automatic sending of a message to new followers.

Let's go to Settings> Follower DM to set an automatic message to send to those who follow us, whether they come from Stim Social or other sources. We can use this message to introduce ourselves, to tell what we offer and in general to start a conversation of any kind.

Case Study: Mercedes GLA

Finally, we see a very particular way of using Instagram, designed by Mercedes-Benz for the Mercedes GLA.

What Mercedes has done is to use the tags in the photos to create a real car customization system. It has created many profiles on Instagram to cover all the possible variants and tag, from time to time, the profile relating to the choice made on the photos.

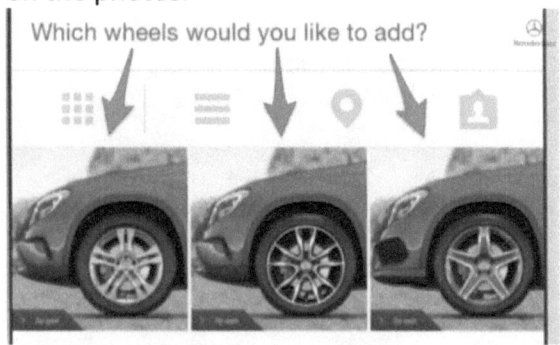

Case Study: AirBNB

Airbnb, the famous house-sharing service, has used a very interesting technique to get, for free, the content to be published in its Instagram Stories.

As we have seen in the course of this book, he has had it created directly by users.

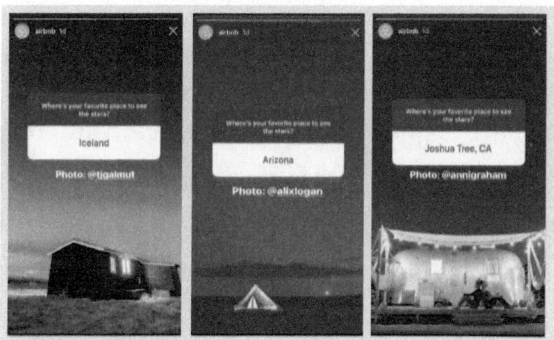

Credit: Later.com

Thus, Airbnb asks all users to take a picture with a particular theme, such as a starry sky.

Then, periodically publish an Instagram Story with the photos that are selected, writing the place and tagging the user.

This generates a chain reaction because even those who did not know about this initiative could be interested in discovering it directly from the Stories that are published.

The result is very effective and allows AirBNB to publish a large number of stories on the same theme. Impressive, and the operation was a success.

Disclaimer

All registered trademarks and logos mentioned in this book, including Amazon and Instagram, belong to their respective owners.

The author of this book does not claim or declare any rights to these trademarks, which are mentioned only for educational and informational purposes.

www.ingramcontent.com/pod-product-compliance
Lightning Source LLC
Chambersburg PA
CBHW020612220526
45463CB00006B/2564